Skills Map

Unit 1 — About presentations
Familiarise yourself with the process of preparing to give a presentation.

Unit 2 — Group presentations
Learn the specific skills needed for giving a group presentation.

Unit 3 — Content
Plan the topic, focus and content of a presentation.

Unit 4 — Communication
Learn the language and delivery skills needed for a competent and confident performance.

Unit 5 — Visual aids
Explore the use of visual aids to appropriately support and enhance main points.

Unit 6 — Slideshow tutorial
Familiarise yourself with presentation software in order to prepare a series of slides.

Destination: Presentations

About presentations

At the end of this unit you will be able to:
- **recognise what makes a good presentation;**
- **understand the process of preparing a presentation.**

Task 1 What makes a good presentation?

A presentation is essentially a talk given to share information with other people. You have probably had many experiences of different kinds of presentations (both academic and non-academic) in your life.

1.1 Think about the presentations you have given or listened to in the past.

Consider as many different aspects of a presentation as possible (for example, the speaker, the topic, the material, the language) and discuss the following questions in groups of three to five.

a) What makes a good presentation?

b) What makes a bad presentation?

1.2 Presentations benefit from good preparation. Now work in pairs and think about the process of preparing a presentation. In your notebook, write a list of the steps you will need to go through from the beginning of the process to the finished product (the final presentation).

Task 2 Planning check list

Compare your answers to Task 1.2 with the following check list. Tick the tasks that you thought of.

Planning check list

Choose your topic In some cases, the topic will be given to you by your tutor. If not, check that it is appropriate with your tutor before the next step.	
Check that you understand the grading criteria Check that you know what is expected of you.	
Conduct research Research will help you know enough about your topic for the presentation. Think about where you can find the information you need (the library, the Internet). References to the sources you have used should be included in a bibliography. This can appear as a final slide in a slideshow or as a handout.	

Decide on a specific focus It is advisable to avoid a general speech, such as, 'All we know about …'. Remember what you are trying to show or prove. Focus the topic to a manageable number of main points.	
Plan what you are going to say Write notes to help you remember the main points of your talk. You should not, however, just read from a script.	
Choose and prepare visual aids Which visual aids will help you communicate your message best?	

Task 3 Grading criteria

If your presentation is going to be assessed, you should find out in advance what assessment criteria will be used. This will help you to plan and give a more effective presentation.

Presentation feedback

Name..

Topic:

Please write your comments in the boxes provided

Clarity:

Organisation:

Fluency:

Visual aids:

3.1 Make a list below of the major criteria you think could be used to assess a presentation. You could use the Planning check list from Task 2 as a guide.

- Organisation: The presentation is well planned and has a clear and logical structure.

Reflect

Look at the criteria for a good presentation again, and think about how these apply to you. Reflect on the following three areas:

- What are your strengths when speaking in front of a group?

- What aspects of presentation-giving could you realistically improve in the short term?

- What aspects of presentation-giving should you allow a longer time to improve?

Student notes for Unit 1

Unit 2 Group presentations

At the end of this unit you will:
- understand how to organise the preparation process;
- have a clear idea about individual roles and responsibilities.

You will sometimes be expected to give a presentation as a member of a group. In this unit you will explore the dynamics of group presentations and then work with some other students to prepare a presentation on an academic topic. Your tutor will help you decide on this topic. Then, for the rest of this module, you will use the tasks in each unit to help you plan and present your talk together. If you would like more information on teamwork, you can refer to the TASK Team-Working module.

Task 1 Advantages and disadvantages

Work in groups of three to five. Discuss the following questions and make notes.

a) What are the advantages of giving a group presentation?

b) What are the disadvantages of giving a group presentation?

Task 2 Working together

Remember that a group presentation involves team effort. It is always clear to the tutor when students do not work with their group, as their pieces of the presentation do not fit together with the other group members' pieces on the day of delivery.

2.1 Work in your presentation group. Look back at the Planning check list from Unit 1, Task 2, and discuss which of the tasks you should work on as a team and which ones could be done individually. Write your answers in the table on page 8. (You may also decide that some tasks should be tackled individually first and then discussed in a group.)

Team tasks	Individual tasks

2.2 Would the following activities be team tasks or individual tasks? Add them to the table.

- Plan who will do or say what
- Set deadlines
- Select a team coordinator
- Organise a series of meetings for team members
- Rehearse the presentation

Task 3 Group work

Use your Planning check list to get organised and prepare your talk. Remember that you should share the work equally. Arrange to meet the other members of your group at least three times outside of class time to plan and practise your presentation before the final delivery.

It is important to keep a record of the planning for your presentation. If your group presentation is going to be assessed, these records will contribute towards the marks that you are awarded.

3.1 Your first step is to arrange a meeting with your group to agree how you are to proceed. Organise your meeting times using Table 3.1.

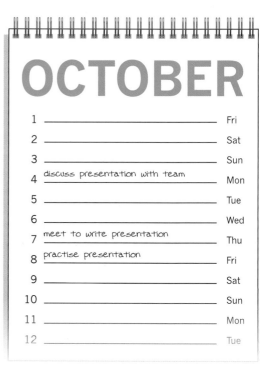

OCTOBER

1	_____	Fri
2	_____	Sat
3	_____	Sun
4	discuss presentation with team	Mon
5	_____	Tue
6	_____	Wed
7	meet to write presentation	Thu
8	practise presentation	Fri
9	_____	Sat
10	_____	Sun
11	_____	Mon
12	_____	Tue

Table 3.1: Meeting information

	Place	Time	Purpose
Meeting 1			
Meeting 2			
Meeting 3			
Meeting 4			

3.2   You should also keep a record of attendance at the meetings.

Table 3.2: Attendance record

Team member's name	E-mail	Phone number	Meeting attendance			
			M1	M2	M3	M4

It will also aid your organisation if you keep a record in note form of what was discussed and what was agreed at your meetings. The individual members of your group could take it in turns to take these notes and then distribute them to the other members.

Task 4 Sharing responsibilities

It is important that every member of the group takes responsibility for the preparation of your presentation.

Record who is responsible for each task in the grid on page 10. This will ensure that the work is shared equally and that nothing is forgotten.

Table 4.1: Actions and responsibilities

Name	Responsibility	Action

Reflect

Think about why it is essential for members of a group to rehearse their presentation together.

Do you feel that you played an appropriate role in planning the presentation?

Could you have done anything differently?

Student notes for Unit 2

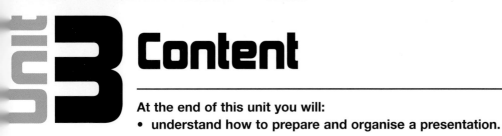

Unit 3 Content

At the end of this unit you will:
- understand how to prepare and organise a presentation.

Task 1 A short presentation

1.1　Imagine you are giving a talk on 'How to deliver an effective presentation'. In groups, discuss what you would include in your presentation.

1.2　Write the characteristics of a good presentation as a series of bullet points.

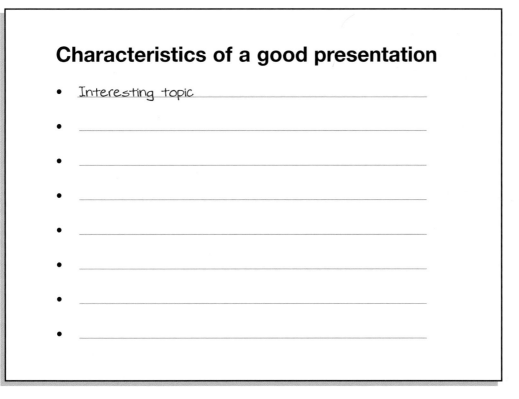

Characteristics of a good presentation

- Interesting topic
-
-
-
-
-
-
-

1.3　Compare your answers with another student. Were your bullet points similar or different? Add any ideas that you agree with to your list.

1.4　Work in groups. Use your bullet point notes as the basis of a brief presentation to your group. Try to speak spontaneously on the basis of each point you have on the list.

1.5　Discuss the structure of the presentations you have just given as a class. How did you feel about the structure and organisation? Did you feel that there was a clear beginning, middle and end?

Task 2 Introduction to planning

Each presentation group should have agreed on a topic and completed the necessary research. It is now time to plan what you are going to say by preparing the content in a clear and logical way. This will enable your audience to both engage with your presentation and recall what you have said.

2.1   Study the diagram and be ready to explain the structure of a presentation to the rest of the class.

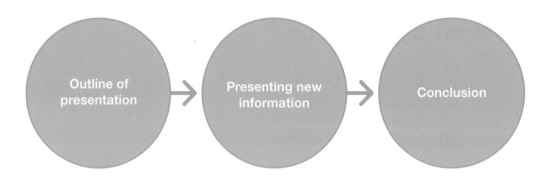

2.2   In your presentation groups, give a brief overview to the rest of the class of the following:

- the topic of your presentation;
- the main points of your presentation.

Task 3 Planning your presentation

3.1   Continue in your presentation group and plan your introduction. Answer the three questions below together to create an introduction that you feel will get the attention of your audience. Make sure that one of the members in your group keeps a clear record of the points you make.

Introduce yourself and your topic:

How will you address the audience and what will you tell them about yourself?

What is your topic and why have you chosen it?

Thesis:

What research question are you going to answer in this presentation?

3.2   Continue in your presentation group. Think about the main points that you would like to make. These should be closely related to your thesis. For each main point, give some support; this could be detail, explanation or evidence. If contrasting opinions exist, make sure you consider both sides of the argument.

Make sure that one member of the group keeps a record under the following headings:

first main point:

   Support:

Second main point:

   Support:

Third main point:

   Support:

fourth main point:

   Support:

3.3   The conclusion should describe clearly what your presentation has shown.

As your conclusion is the final thing your audience will hear, it is particularly important that it should make an impact. For example, when you go over points you have already made in the main body, make sure you do this clearly and concisely without simply repeating what you have said before.

Work on your conclusions in your presentation group. Then present your conclusions to the class.

3.4   It is useful to prepare a bibliography to hand out to the audience after your presentation. Make a list of the sources (books, websites, journal articles, etc.) you used to support your points/arguments.

Task 4 Preparing notes

Giving a presentation is not the same as reading an essay out loud. This is why it is useful to write your presentation in note form rather than continuous prose. You should already know what you want to say; the notes just provide a framework so you can keep to the structure you have planned.

4.1   Discuss in groups the presentation you did in Task 1. How did you find using the bullet point notes?

4.2   In your presentation groups, use the information from Task 3 to write your own set of notes. Take account of anything you have learned from the discussion in Task 4.1.

Reflect

Think about the outline plan you made for your presentation.

What helped you to organise your ideas?

How are the preparation stages for a presentation similar to or different from those of planning an essay?

Student notes for Unit 3

Unit 4 Communication

At the end of this unit you will be:
- more familiar with the language of presentations;
- able to use appropriate body language.

Once you have researched and prepared the content of a talk, it is essential to focus on its delivery.

Task 1 The language of presentations

The language you use can help indicate the structure of your presentation and guide the audience.

1.1 Match the functions a–e below with the appropriate groups of phrases 1–5 underneath. These phrases are known as signposts because they help to clarify where your presentation is going. The first one has been done for you as an example.

a) __2__ Introducing your presentation

b) _____ Outlining what you are going to say

c) _____ Making your first point

d) _____ Adding more points

e) _____ Closing

1
- Finally, I would like to turn to …
- My final point is with regard to …

2
- My presentation today concerns …
- I would like to talk to you today about …

3
- To begin with …
- Turning then to the first point …

4
- I shall be looking at the following areas:
- I have divided my talk into the following areas:

5
- My next point concerns …
- That brings me to …
- I want to turn now to … / I'd like to turn now to …

1.2 Similar phrases can be used to signal when you are doing other things within each stage of your presentation. Match the functions f–j to the phrases 6–10 below.

f) .... Giving emphasis (for example, in your conclusion)

g) .... Adding more information

h) .... Making a generalisation

i) .... Balancing an argument, stating opposing views

j) .... Giving an example

6
- It must be remembered that …
- It should be emphasised that …
- I would like to underline the point that …

7
- To illustrate this point, …
- For instance, …
- A good example of this is …

8
- In addition, …
- Furthermore, …
- Not only … but also …
- I should add that …

9
- On the whole, …
- Generally speaking, …

10
- On the one hand … but on the other hand …

Task 2 Delivering a presentation

In addition to your command of English, your body language will also affect how your presentation is received. Some of the things that speakers often do during a presentation are listed below.

2.1 With a partner, discuss what impression each one may give the audience. Can you add anything to the list?

- smile at the audience
- sit down
- walk around
- look only at notes
- use hand gestures
- play with hair/change in pocket/earring, etc.

- lean against a wall
- point at the audience
-
-
-
-

2.2 Body language is not universal. If your body language and gestures are misinterpreted, it can result in confusion. Discuss the following questions in groups of three to five.

a) What sort of differences have you noticed in the way that people from other cultures use gestures and body language?

b) Have you ever experienced a communication breakdown due to a misunderstanding about the meaning of a gesture?

Reflect

Think about occasions in the past when you have had to speak in front of an audience or speak in a stressful situation, for example at an interview. Try to remember the kind of language you used and what your body language communicated about yourself.

Now think about the changes in your language and body language that you feel will be useful for you in future formal speaking situations. Refer back to some of the ideas in this unit.

Student notes for Unit 4

Unit 5 Visual aids

At the end of this unit you will be:
- more familiar with a range of appropriate visual aids;
- able to use visual aids effectively.

Visual aids can greatly enhance an oral presentation by highlighting key points or information and helping the audience to understand the information.

Task 1 Choosing and using visual aids

There are many kinds of visual aids available. Think about presentations and lectures you have attended in the past and consider the visual aids that were used.

1.1 Discuss with another student which of the following you have either seen or used. What do you think are the advantages and disadvantages of each of them, for the audience and/or for the speaker?

Visual aid	Advantages	Disadvantages
Posters		
Overhead transparencies		
Videos		
Whiteboard		
Printed handouts		
PowerPoint slides		

1.2 Visual aids are useful to help get your message across to your audience. Nevertheless, even with good visual aids, things can go wrong if they are not used appropriately. Look at the list of 'don'ts' below and discuss why each point is a problem.

DON'T:

- crowd too much information into one visual

- put unimportant details in the visual

- forget to talk about information in a visual

- use 12-point font or less

- put visuals in a different order to that of information in the presentation

Task 2 Preparation of visual aids

Once you have chosen (or been assigned) a particular visual aid for your presentation, it is important to be clear on the preparation that will be involved.

The following example indicates seven questions you should ask yourself in order to prepare any visual aid. If you can answer each question with confidence, then you know what you have to do.

In the example, the questions have been applied to giving a poster presentation, as this is a popular visual aid and it is quite likely you will present or view posters while you are a student.

Question	Answer
a) What visual aid am I going to use?	Poster presentation
b) What is it?	A poster is a large document (usually mounted on a card backing) that can be used to communicate your research at a presentation or meeting. A poster usually contains both text and pictures/graphs. The presenter generally stands next to his/her poster ready to answer questions as people pass by and read what it says.
c) Are there any special requirements or constraints?	Make sure you know the size of the poster you are expected to produce, as this is usually set in advance.
d) What materials/ equipment do I need?	• backing card or poster board cut to the required size • A4 paper • glue and scissors
e) How will the content be organised?	A poster presentation is one large document that is generally subdivided into some or all of the following sections: • Title • Introduction • Methods • Results • Discussion • Conclusion • References
f) What is the best layout?	A poster has to be legible from a distance, so the most important advice here is to have limited text and interesting graphics. Techniques are: • use short sentences and bullets • use large font size • use pictures, charts and graphs to illustrate information • use colour carefully to add interest
g) How do I put it all together?	The easiest way is to print out each section of your poster on A4 paper and place these smaller elements of the poster into position on the backing. This method allows more flexibility in design, as you can move sections around until you are happy with the results. Here is one possible layout: ┌──────────────────────────┐ │ Title │ ├────────┬─────────┬───────┤ │Introduc-│Graphs/ │Conclu-│ │tion │pictures │sion │ └────────┴─────────┴───────┘

2.1 Work with a partner and choose another type of visual aid from the table in Task 1.1. Apply the same seven questions to the visual aid and fill in the table below.

Question	Answer
a) What visual aid am I going to use?	
b) What is it?	
c) Are there any special requirements or constraints?	
d) What materials/equipment do I need?	
e) How will the content be organised?	
f) What is the best layout?	
g) How do I put it all together?	

2.2   Work with another pair who chose a different type of visual aid. Swap information about the visual aids you chose to think about. Fill in the table below with your new partners' information.

Question	Answer
a) What visual aid am I going to use?	
b) What is it?	
c) Are there any special requirements or constraints?	
d) What materials/equipment do I need?	
e) How will the content be organised?	
f) What is the best layout?	
g) How do I put it all together?	

Reflect

Choose one or two situations where visual aids have been used for your benefit, whether at school or at other kinds of presentations. Try to remember how you felt about the use of the visual aids and whether they were beneficial to the overall learning experience.

Apply anything you have gained from your reflections to your own presentation. For example, what problems might you have with the type of visual aid you have chosen?

Think about how you could prepare a back-up plan if things go wrong with the visual element of your presentation.

Student notes for Unit 5

Slideshow tutorial

At the end of this unit you will be able to:
- make a slideshow;
- understand how a slideshow can help you to get your message across.

Use of ICT (Information and Communication Technology) for the purpose of presentations is now commonplace, both in the classroom and in the world of work. An understanding of how to make use of slideshow software can greatly enhance the delivery of a presentation. Use the following 10-step guide to familiarise yourself with the process of creating presentation slides.

Step 1: Opening a new slide show

First, open your slideshow software package by clicking on its icon on your desktop or selecting the program from the 'Start' menu. It's a good idea to make it a habit to save your presentation often by selecting 'Save' from the 'File' menu at the top of your document.

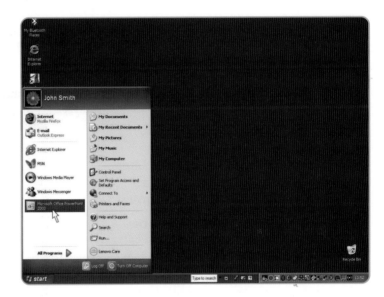

Step 2: Creating your slides

When you first open your software, a blank page may appear. If this is what happens, go straight to Step 3.

Alternatively, you may be asked to select a page from an 'Auto Layout' screen. This enables you to choose the structure of your slide(s) from a range of options. If you are asked to choose from the 'Auto Layout' screen, choose the slide in the top left-hand corner. You will be able to experiment with alternatives after completing this tutorial.

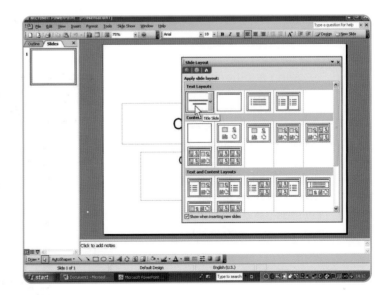

Step 3: Adding text

On the main screen, follow the
instructions 'Click to add title' and
'Click to add subtitle'. These guide
you through the process of creating
a basic text slide.

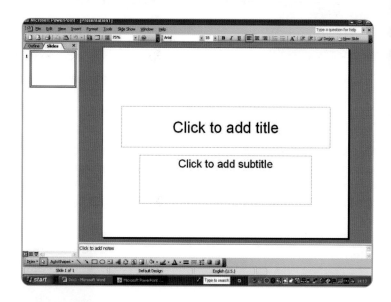

Step 4: Adding design features

To create a more advanced slide
with more sophisticated design
features, click on the 'Design' button
at the top of your screen or select
'Slide Design' from the 'Format' menu.

A variety of design options will be
displayed on the right of your
screen. You will then be able to
choose a style template with
different colours and images from
a series of predesigned templates.
This will help you to personalise
your presentation.

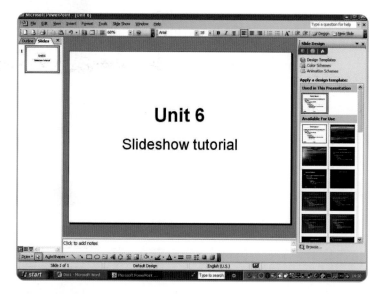

Step 5: Adding additional slides

To create additional slides, click on
the 'New Slide' button on your
toolbar, or select 'New Slide' from the
'Insert' menu. This will create an
additional slide. You may also be
asked to choose the layout of your
new slide using the 'Auto Layout'
menu, as indicated in Step 2 above.

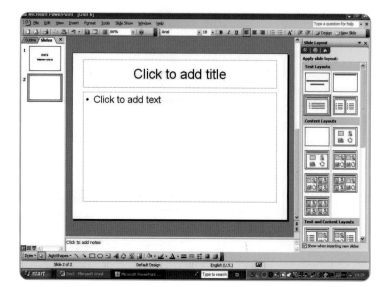

Step 6: Reordering your slides

If necessary, you can change the order of your slides by clicking and dragging the smaller versions of the slides which appear on the left-hand side of your screen.

Step 7: Adding pictures

In addition to the use of text, your software also allows you to insert pictures to improve the appearance of your slides. There are two main methods of finding and inserting images.

Method 1: Internet images
Copying and pasting images from the Internet can be an effective way to increase the impact of your slides. First, find a web page with a suitable image. Next, place your mouse pointer over the image and click the right-hand button on the mouse. Then select 'Copy'. Finally, go back to your slideshow software and select 'Paste' from the 'Edit' toolbar. The image should then appear in your presentation slides. Don't forget to acknowledge the source of the image. Cut and paste the web address of the image under the image on your slide.

Method 2: Clip art
In addition to the images which are available on the Internet, your software will also contain a series of images stored in an area called 'Clip Art'. You can access 'Clip Art' by clicking on the 'Insert' menu on the toolbar at the top of your screen. You will then be able to search for relevant pictures using key words. If a suitable picture is available, you can then click on the image and it will appear in your presentation.

Step 8: Using animation

To control the way in which text and images first appear on your slides, a variety of animation effects can be used.

Select 'Animation Schemes' from the 'Slide Show' menu in the toolbar at the top of your screen. You will then be presented with a range of different animation choices. You can experiment with these by clicking on the different text and image elements of your presentation and choosing a suitable animation for that element. You can test the animation to see what it looks like by clicking on the 'Play' button.

Step 9: Viewing your presentation

To see what your finished presentation will look like when it is shown to your audience, you will need to select the 'View Show' option from the 'Slide Show' menu. 'View Show' displays your slides to their best advantage, using the full screen.

Step 10: Printing your presentation

To print copies of your slides onto paper or onto overhead projector transparencies, choose 'Print ...' from the 'File' menu of the toolbar at the top of your screen. You will then be able to choose whether to print full slides or smaller versions of your slides for use as handouts or notes.

Reflect

Ask your tutor for more information about the presentations that you will have to give during your current course of study. Plan ahead and start to think about how the available software could help to enhance your delivery.

If you decide to use computer technology, think about the preparation you will need to make, for example: check that the room in which you will give your presentation has the appropriate facilities and that you know how to use the facilities before the day of your presentation.

Student notes for Unit 6

Module 11

Web work

Website 1   **Presentation planner**

http://elc.polyu.edu.hk/cill/tools/presplan.htm

Review

This website is designed to help you plan, organise and write your presentation by following a series of prompts. It will also provide note cards and a script of your finished product, and a record of what your presentation will sound like.

Task

Once you have a finished presentation, use this presentation planner to do a test run of your talk. If you are pleased with the finished result, take advantage of the option of printing out note cards.

Website 2   **PowerPoint in the classroom**

http://www.actden.com/pp/

Review

The tutorial takes you through all the steps in creating and editing PowerPoint slides.

Task

If you still feel that you need more help with PowerPoint, try the tutorial offered here.

Extension activities

Activity 1   **PowerPoint practice**

Practise your PowerPoint skills by making slides to illustrate the key steps of the Planning check list in Unit 1.

Look back at the Planning check list in Unit 1 and make PowerPoint slides to give a short presentation of this information. What information would you include on the slide, and what would you say to illustrate the main point?

Compare your work with another student. Have you handled the check list in similar ways?

Activity 2 — Presenting research

Some presentations require you to conduct your own research and then present the results to your class. In this activity, you will give a presentation detailing the results of a short questionnaire on student attitudes to a particular aspect of university life, e.g., exams, seminars, oral presentations, note-taking.

There are several parts to the activity:

1 Design a short questionnaire to find out information about students' attitudes to the aspect of university life that you have chosen.

You could include questions on:

- Extent of experience with …

- Views on advantages and disadvantages of …

- Self-rating of skill at …

- Opinion of usefulness of … skills beyond university

2 Obtain responses from at least 10 other students.

3 Compile your results and share them with the rest of your class in a presentation with visual aids.

Glossary

Animation (n) Moving picture images such as cartoons, video or moving diagrams. Animation can be used in *presentations*.

Balance an argument (v) To make sure that both sides of an argument have been considered and explained.

Bibliography (n) A list of *references* to *sources* cited in the text of a piece of academic writing or a book. A bibliography should consist of an alphabetical list of books, papers, journal articles and websites and is usually found at the end of the work. It may also include texts suggested by the author for further reading.

Body language (n) Non-verbal communication of feelings and ideas through movements of the body. For example, certain body movements such as fidgeting and yawning may indicate boredom.

Check list (n) A list of tasks to do or aspects to consider when planning and preparing for an event such as an academic assignment, journey or party.

Communication breakdown (n) A situation in which individuals or groups are unable to understand each other at all due to differences in language, culture or belief.

Constraint (n) Something that places a limit or restriction on what you want to do. For example, if you are doing a *presentation*, there may be time constraints.

Coordinator (n) Someone who is responsible for arranging how a group or workforce shares out duties and for ensuring that the final product or results are brought together effectively.

Deadline (n) The date or time by which something needs to be completed. In academic situations, deadlines are normally given for handing in essays and assignments.

Dynamics (n) The way that things work together to produce energy and results. For example, it is important that group dynamics are effective so that everyone works well together.

Emphasise (v) To highlight or draw attention to something that is important.

Evidence (n) Information and data that establish whether something is true or not.

Framework (n) A basic *structure* that is an *outline* of something more detailed.

Gesture (n) (v) 1 (n) An action meant to communicate an idea nonverbally or to *emphasise* a thought or meaning. 2 (v) To make such an action. For example, putting one's hand over one's heart indicates sincerity.

Grading criteria (n) The basis on which something will be assessed. It is important to know what the grading criteria consist of when writing an academic assignment. For example, a piece of work may be assessed on grammatical accuracy and/or how well it is presented, or it may be evaluated on its content alone.

Handout (n) Paper-based information that is given out by the lecturer or speaker in a lecture, seminar or tutorial. It usually gives a summary, *bibliography* or extra information connected with the lecture topic. It may also be a worksheet.

ICT (also IT) (n) Information and communication technology. Technology, such as computers, *presentation* software, DVD and other media, that helps people to manage information electronically.

Layout (n) The way that things are positioned within a space, for example, the way text, pictures and diagrams are arranged on a page or computer screen.

Outline (n) (v) 1 (n) A rough, often point-form, sketch of the main ideas in a text or *presentation*. 2 (v) To give or make a rough sketch of the main ideas or events in a text or *presentation*.

Overhead transparency (OHT) (n) Clear, plastic film on which text and visuals can be reproduced, enlarged and projected onto a wall or screen using a computer or overhead projector (OHP). This type of *visual aid* is often used during lectures and *presentations*.

Poster presentation (n) A *presentation* that involves displaying posters with information and pictures or diagrams. The audience generally reads the posters while the presenter stands next to them and explains information where necessary.

PowerPoint (n) The brand name for a type of software known as a presentation program. The software enables users to write and design slideshows for *presentations*. The slides may be viewed on computer, projected onto a screen and/or printed out.

Presentation (n) A short lecture, talk or demonstration (usually formal) given in front of an audience. The speaker prepares and *structures* his or her presentation in advance and will often use *visual aids* or realia to illustrate it.

Reference (n) (v) 1 (n) Acknowledgment of the sources of ideas and information that you use in written work and oral *presentations*. 2 (v) To acknowledge or mention *sources* of information.

Rehearse (v) To practise a speech, dialogue, play or *presentation* that is going to be performed in front of an audience.

Research question (n) A statement or question that helps you to start gathering ideas, notes and information in a focused way in preparation for writing an essay, report, *presentation* or dissertation.

Role (n) The part someone plays in a group (or any situation that involves interacting with other people). In some situations, these roles may be flexible or unspoken, in others they are well-defined, such as the leader of a team.

Signposts (n) Words, phrases or other organisational features such as headings and opening sentences in a text that help the audience or reader identify a section. For example, a lecturer may signpost the conclusion of a talk by prefacing it with 'to sum up...'.

Source (n) Something (usually a book, article or other text) that supplies you with information. In an academic context, sources used in *essays* and reports must be acknowledged.

Spontaneous (adj) Describes an action that is taken without preplanning, that is, without prior discussion and rehearsal.

Structure (n) (v) 1 (n) A *framework* or arrangement of several parts, put together in a particular way. 2 (v) In academic terms, to put together ideas or arguments in a logical way for an essay or *presentation*.

Support (n) (v) 1 (n) *Evidence* and ideas that back up an argument. 2 (v) To back up an argument with evidence.

Thesis (n) The controlling idea, main argument or question in a piece of academic writing or a *presentation*. It is stated in the introduction and *supported* by *evidence*.

Visual aid (n) An object or image that is used in a lecture, *presentation* or lesson to help clarify information visually. For example, diagrams, pictures, posters, models and video are commonly used visual aids.

Further notes